Testin

"This book is truly about something that many of us may be curious about but can now have insight into the supernatural from a real psychic. Linda writes about her initial angst at receiving visions, hearing voices, seeing objects as a young child. However through time and learning, she has been able to understand this "gift" and use it to help those who seek her advice, to the best possible advantage. Her journey as described in the first person makes it more powerful to the reader.

For anyone who may be sceptically about psychics, I highly recommend they read Linda's book. "

Jill L. O'Donnell,
President
Author, Trainer, Speaker
IRIS Consulting for Seniors Inc.

"Strange Normal provides a most thought provoking description of phenomena and circumstances that will be of interest to believers and non-believers alike. Linda manages to share with the reader the experience of her spiritual journey in a way that is both uplifting and provocative"

Peter Hoy
Friend and Former Colleague

Strange Normal

(Journey of a Psychic)

Linda Dianne

Copyright © 2011 by Linda Dianne

All rights reserved

No part of this book may be reproduced, stored in a retrieval system, or transmitted by any means, electronic, mechanical, photocopying, recording, or otherwise, without written permission from the author or publisher. There is one exception. Brief passages may be quoted in articles or reviews.

Library and Archives Canada Cataloguing in Publication

Cataloguing data available through Library and Archives Canada

ISBN 978-1-55483-909-4

Acknowledgements

My sincere thanks and appreciation to
the following people:

Jill L.O'Donnell,
President, Author, Trainer, Speaker
IRIS Consulting for Seniors Inc.

Peter Hoy
Friend and Former Colleague

Dorna Revie
Owner of Energy Centre, Geneva,
Switzerland
A recognised Sophrology School
(A Swiss method for optimal health
and well-being)

Their friendship and support are
greatly appreciated.

Contents

The contents of this book, contains some of my personal experiences in communicating with the "Other side" using different mediums. Below is a list of the mediums that were used to communicate with Spirit .

1. Rune Cards

2. Playing Cards

3. Tea leaves

4. Ouija Board

5. Automatic writing

6. Crystal-Gazing (Crystal Ball)

Introduction

As a psychic I have often been asked when I realized that I had this gift, how do I receive messages and knowledge from the other side; and how do I communicate with them and they with me.

In the pages of this book it is my intent to take you on a journey into my world as a psychic by describing some of the readings I have done for clients and how the messages were received and interpreted.

Every psychic has their own way of communicating with Spirit and each have their own technique on giving readings. It takes time to understand and accept the communications. It also takes time to set the boundaries that need to be in place in order to receive messages from Spirit that are accurate and come from God's purest messengers.

As you follow my journey through the pages of this book please take the time to learn from my experiences without judgement but with the sincere intent of this book to enlighten all that are confused about Spirit and the *Strange* but *Normal* life of a psychic.

I chose the title *Strange Normal* for this book for the simple reason that for many the psychic world is strange, confusing and somewhat intimidating and yet fascinating. For psychics communication with Spirit is normal.

When most people visit a psychic they are either at a crossroads in their life, have suffered a loss, or searching for that special someone. They also come when they are depressed, angry and with very low self esteem.

The role of the psychic, as I see it, is not to provide the quick fix answers but to help find the core of what is creating the circumstances that the client is in and to suggest ways (from Spirit) on how to continue their journey here on earth.

Being a psychic is more than someone giving readings. Our lives are often disrupted on many occasions when someone from the other side makes a surprise visit.

14 — Linda Dianne

Chapter One
Communication with the Other side

16 — Linda Dianne

First of all I want to begin by telling you that everyone is psychic. Yes, everyone is psychic. We all have the way and means of communication with the other side, just as we all can communicate with each other here on earth. The difference is that some of us have a stronger talent in doing so. Others may have a stronger talent to sing, or dance, play a musical instrument and so on. I can sing, but certainly not well, and I can dance but am not good at it or comfortable doing so, but the point is that I can sing and dance even though I choose not to. You may not be comfortable with communication with Spirit but it does not mean that you can't communicate. Your strength may be teaching, or athletic or perhaps in the medical profession.

Before we venture onto my psychic journey, let me explain the different ways of communicating with Spirit. Many are familiar with the technique known as *Clairvoyance* through renowned psychics who have written several books and who have appeared on television such as Sylvia Browne, who was often a guest on the Montel Williams show and John Edward who had his own television show. Both of these psychics delivered messages from Spirit to their studio audience at random. *Clairvoyance* (clear seeing) is the ability to receive images in a visual manner such as symbols, pictures and even Spirit in the image of a loved one that has crossed over.

Clairaudience (clear hearing) is the ability to receive messages through sound, usually in your mind's voice and not through your ears. You may have already experienced this and did not associate it with psychic awareness or coming from Spirit. Sometimes a powerful thought will penetrate and guide you either out of danger or to a destination to keep you from being lost. Or you may simply receive a great idea or a solution to a problem that has been bothering you. Although you may not have heard a voice/sound in your head you did hear your own voice as you received the message/thought as if reading silently to yourself.

Clairsentience (clear sensing) is the ability to sense and feel information. This is commonly referred to as "gut feeling" often portrayed by police agencies in television programs, books and in films when solving cases using their gut instincts. You have probably experienced emotions of fear, sudden chills ("goose bumps"), the hair on the back of your neck rising, tingling sensations, sympathetic and empathetic pain. You may have instinctively known that a certain environment you entered did not give you a good feeling and made you uncomfortable. This is <u>feeling</u> information and the information is coming from Spirit to protect you.

Clairalience (clear smelling) is the ability to receive communication from Spirit through the sense of smell. You may have suddenly smelt the wonderful scent of a bouquet of flowers, perfume, smoke, baking, freshly baked bread, leather and even coffee. As fast as the scent arrives it disappears. This is a communication from the other side, perhaps from a loved one just letting you know they are still with you by sending a scent that would be associated with them when they lived on earth.

Clairambience (clear tasting) is the ability to receive communication through a taste in your mouth. Usually the taste is of a favourite food or one that has significance to the person communicating with you. Some psychics/mediums will use this ability to help solve criminal cases by experiencing and identifying perhaps the taste of certain substances such as gasoline, sand, smoke, and so on that may have been used while a crime was being committed by the means of suffocation.

Psychic information or communication with Spirit is accessed through the *Clairs* and the information received is processed with our conscious mind.

For me, *clairvoyance* (clear seeing) and *clairaudience* (clear hearing) are my greatest strengths but I also can and do communicate with the other side through automatic writing and through *Clairsentience* (clear sensing).

22 — Linda Dianne

Chapter Two
The Zodiac Signs

24 — Linda Dianne

From the viewpoint of earth the Sun appears to move along a circular orbit across the *celestial sphere*. This circular orbit is called the ecliptic. The Zodiac refers to the thin band along the ecliptic composed of the zodiac signs and constellations. The zodiac is divided into twelve different signs each of which is 30 degrees long and begins at Aries. It is believed that the concept of the zodiac evolved from Babylonian astronomy.

The order of the zodiac signs is Aries, Taurus, Gemini, Cancer, Leo, Virgo, Libra, Scorpio, Sagittarius, Capricorn, Aquarius and Pisces. Astrological signs represent twelve equal segments or divisions of the Zodiac. According to astrology, celestial phenomena govern human activity on the principle of *"as above, so below"*. The twelve signs represent twelve basic personality types or characteristic modes of expression. There are sun signs and moon signs, which both depend on your date of birth.

During ancient times, the passage of the sun was monitored because it was useful in predicting the change of seasons. Over time, however, people began to associate the zodiac sign, or Sun's position in the zodiac, with birth dates and characteristics.

My first conscious awareness of communication with Spirit was through my grandmother, my mother's mother, who was interested in astrology and read tea leaves and cards.

When I was about 9 or 10 my grandmother introduced my siblings and me to this wonderful, fascinating world of receiving information from another source. An invisible source or an imaginary source as it was to us at the time. This gift or talent was then referred to as *Fortune Telling*. The words Spirit or psychic were never mentioned.

My grandmother did readings for fun, entertainment and for charity. Although she was the kind of grandmother that baked, hugged, and made Sunday's special when we dined at her place; and she made afternoon tea a tradition and sometimes followed it up with the reading of the tea leaves and eventually on occasion the reading of the cards. My grandmother did readings for fun, entertainment and for charity. Although she was very accurate in the information she provided she seldom spoke of her abilities and silently and carefully provided information as necessary. She taught us the signs of the Zodiac and introduced us to the horoscope world and the information found amongst the stars.

We all knew our Zodiac Sign and the characteristics associated with each sign. As my birthday is December 2nd, I learned that I am a Sagittarius "the Archer". This Zodiac sign is for those born from November 24th to December

21st. My grandmother was also a Sagittarius born on December 4th.

I would read my horoscope with great interest and tried to adapt to all the characteristics a Sagittarius was supposed to have. At an early age I didn't quite live up to all the characteristics listed but I wasn't worried I knew I would eventually be a real honest to goodness Sagittarius and I was on my journey to make sure this happened.

It didn't happen! I learned much later in my teens that you don't necessarily need to acquire all the characteristics of the Zodiac sign you are born under. You only just need to be aware of how different and how much the same people born under the same sign are. Yes different and the same. Different in that everyone born under the same Zodiac sign does not resemble each other in appearance, intelligence, size, shape and profession. *Same* in that everyone is unique and special and wonderful, and may have similar thought processes and interests.

I learned that the planets in order in which they exert their influence play an important role on our lives. I read that I should marry a person born under the sign of Leo, Sagittarius or Aries. My best day will be Tuesday. My lucky colours are green and purple; and my lucky gems are the turquoise and the moonstone. I also learned that Sagittarians love animals, and the outdoors and nature. They love to travel, have many friends and are very creative.

What I am going to tell you next will make you question, as I have done, as to the reality of me being born under the sign of Sagittarius.

I absolutely dislike camping and hiking, and do not have a fondness for animals or the outdoors. I would never hurt an animal but I also would not have one as a pet. I do however love to travel and stay in nice hotels. Whether they are lucky or not my favourite colour is pink and I am fond of the colour purple.

Turquoise is my birth gemstone, and I do like it, however, give me a diamond any day and I will proudly wear it.

My first marriage was to a man born under the sign of the Capricorn. Perhaps I should have taken the advice given to marry a Leo, Sagittarius or Aries. My second and final marriage is to a wonderful man born under the Zodiac sign of Aries (glad I did that right). As for my best day being Tuesday, I think each day is a good day and give thanks to God for another day to learn and share and love.

As for friends, I am honestly blessed with many wonderful people in my life. Creative, is indeed a Sagittarian trait that I have.

Chapter Three
Communication with Spirit

My first realization of my own experience with the unseen world, and receiving a message from Spirit was after witnessing the tragic death of my youngest sister. I was 12 at the time and my psychic journey as I know it begins here.

The details of my sister's death are written in my first book *"Hugs From Heaven"*, so I will spare you the details of her death and continue from that day onto the path of psychic awareness and the incredible journey that follows.

I have always known that there was something guiding and protecting me, and believed that they were from the universe somewhere out there beyond the clouds. I believe that God is the creator of all things and it was God that was sending me protection and guidance.

On the night that my sister passed away, I felt a feeling of peace and love. Not because she was gone, but this was an awareness that I was going to be fine. I heard a soft sweet voice in my head tell me that she was ok and it was her time to leave us. I felt comfort and love and somehow knew that this was something that I needed to go through. How I knew was a mystery to me then, but I realize now that witnessing this tragic event opened a communication with the other side that for me was totally unexpected.

At first I just seem to know things and there was no logical way of me knowing. I could sense energies around me and I knew when someone was there even though they were not visible. I didn't tell anyone for fear of being treated differently. I didn't even tell my grandmother whom I'm sure would have understood and perhaps helped me deal with it.

I even tried desperately to ignore the information I was receiving and pretend that I didn't sense the energies around me. I didn't know what to do with this sudden change in my mind and in the way that I saw things. I didn't understand why, when things happened it didn't disturb me the way it did others. I always knew that things would be fine. I always saw things differently and my thinking was different than my siblings and friends.

Through my teenage years I began to find comfort in daydreaming, and looking up into the sky and identifying the different shapes the clouds made. This exercise helped me later on when I began to read tea leaves. The shapes of the clouds kept changing and I would creatively make up a story to go with whatever the cloud represented.

One day, I saw more than the clouds, I saw the shape of an Angel. It wasn't a cloud, but a mist that formed right in front of me and an arm reached out to touch my cheek. And I felt the gentle sweep of the hand touch me and tingling sensations flowed through my body. Was I dreaming? Did this really happen? For days I saw the image of the Angel in my mind's eye. I felt the touch of my cheek, it was real.

Knowing that I had an Angel looking out for me was amazing. Me with an Angel! I learned later on that we all have Guardian Angels looking after us, and we all have Spirit Guides guiding us as we go through each stage of our life here on earth.

My family often played card games. We would take turns shuffling the deck of cards and distributing the cards appropriately to each player. Once when we were playing cards I began to have visions. Unexplained visions were forming in my mind like a ticker tape of pictures speeding constantly across my mind. I had no way of knowing what was happening, or how to stop it. I was picking up energies from everyone at the card table and like a mini motion picture images were filling my mind. I thought I was having some kind of brain trauma where things get mixed up and you don't know who you are or where you are. But I did know who I was and where I was and the only thing I didn't know was what was happening to me.

These visions seem to stop after that card game, and I almost completely forgot the incident until a few years later when I was playing a game of solitaire while my infant son slept after his feeding. There I was, quietly spreading the cards on the table and like a sudden bolt of lightning the visions came in such a speed that I couldn't identify what they were.

All I could think about was my baby in the other room. What if something happened to me? My husband wouldn't be home for a few hours and I had no way of knowing what was happening to me, but I did know that I could ask for help. And I did.

I looked towards heaven and called out for help. I just asked for it. It was that simple. I said I needed someone to help me, and protect my baby. "Please tend to me now, protect my baby and help me understand what is happening to me."

The visions stopped immediately and stillness was all around me. I asked for protection and I asked for guidance. I went to my son's room and watched him carefully while he slept. He was fine. I was fine. We were protected. We were safe.

That evening I prayed to God and asked for a sign or something as to what I was supposed to do with the visions I was receiving. "If you want me to help someone I will, but I need to know what it is I am to do." I then called out for the Angel that had touched me in my early years. Are you still with me I called out? Help me please! Tell me what to do!

Help me understand. What am I supposed to do with the visions? They are coming at me too fast, like a bullet whizzing by, and I can't see them clearly. What are the visions for? Why do I need them? Please help me!

And the answer soon came. Not that evening, not even that week, but a few days later my Angel appeared before me again. And like before the Angel touched my cheek and then disappeared. My body was at peace and my mind was receiving messages and images in a manner that I could understand. I was asked to help others by using the gift of psychic abilities to guide and comfort all that cross my threshold. I will be guided and protected. All I have to do is ask for guidance and protection.

This didn't mean that I had to do readings for everyone that visited me and it didn't mean that I could look into their lives and know their dark secrets. This is not what being psychic is. What I was asked to do was help others using my psychic strengths whenever I could.

I wasn't about to announce to the world or to anyone that I am psychic. I wasn't ready for that. I still had to find out what it all meant and I had to be comfortable in tapping into the universal information source on a regular basis. I had to adapt to ways of communicating with the Spirit world without bringing attention to myself.

For the next 30 years I silently and carefully communicated with Spirit when I needed information on how to help the people that I came into contact with. Not everyone needed help, and certainly I wasn't some kind of "Wonder Woman" God chose to solve the problems of others. I am psychic not someone that can magically make everyone's life better. Sometimes it just required me to listen, to smile, to take someone to an appointment. When someone sought council from me as a friend it was Spirit that guided my words and actions.

My very dear friends have only recently found out that I am psychic. Some of them have been my friend since the age of 6, and others for almost 40 years. They had no way of knowing my secret life and I wasn't comfortable on letting them in or knowing information about them that could put a strain on our relationship. I didn't want them to feel uncomfortable around me perhaps thinking that I could read their minds or that I was viewing their lives.

It is a great comfort to me to know that my friends are my friends because they truly like and respect me and not for any other reason.

42 — *Linda Dianne*

Chapter Four
A Psychic Beacon

44 — Linda Dianne

There is a price to pay when you don't protect yourself every day and I found out the hard way. I thought that I only needed to ask for protection when I was contacting Spirit. I was wrong. I need to ask for protection every day because when you are psychic you automatically become like a beacon for all Spirits, good and bad, that have the ability to attach them self to you and eventually cause great harm.

My vibrations were sending out light that was reaching the Spirit realm like an invitation to enter my space. All of us have our own vibration frequencies that send signals into the universe. Vibrations are strongest when Consciousness and our vibration frequency are perfectly correlated. Simply stated when you're lower in frequency, you're lower in consciousness and your perception is dulled as if you view things through a foggy lens. When you're higher in frequency, you're higher in consciousness, your perception is heightened and you see things more clearly the higher you go. Just as when you ascend in an airplane, you see a larger picture the higher you climb, and the brighter it becomes as you break through the clouds.

The higher your vibration frequency is, the more you are able to comprehend because you are allowing a greater *Flow of Life Force* through your mind and body. Our vibration frequency depends on the amount of *Life Force* we are channelling through us. *Life Force* is also known as "God Energy and Intelligence." Another word for this phenomenon is Love, which is the essence of Source, and is continually emanating from Source.

The more you allow the essence of the Creator to flow through your mind and body, the higher you are in vibration frequency. The lower you are in vibration frequency, the less creative ideas and empowerment you experience and can utilize.

One incident that happened to me when I didn't ask for protection was when I was attending an event held in one of the museums in Toronto. When I left work and headed for the museum it never occurred to me to ask for protection. I was attending an event not contacting Spirit, or so I thought.

The event took place during one of the winter months. I was heading towards the stairway that led to the cloak room to dispose of my coat. I noticed an elderly woman at the top of the stairs. I thought that she was waiting for someone so I began to descend the stairs towards the cloak room. As I placed my foot on the second step I felt a thump on my lower back. It was a pressure so incredibly strong that it forced my body down the stairs to the landing at the end of the stairway. I hit every step on the way down and somehow I wasn't injured. However, I was startled, confused and embarrassed.

Two people came to help me up from the floor and to make sure I was alright. I asked if the elderly woman that I had seen at the top of the stairs was alright. They never saw an elderly woman at any time at the top of the stairs and said that they saw me fall and thought that I had perhaps caught the heel of my shoe on the bottom of my coat and it triggered the fall. I agreed with them that my fall probably happened that way. But I know it didn't.

That same elderly woman appeared in front of me again during the event. This time I asked for protection. I tightened my grip and folded my hands into fists ready to protect myself from another physical attack and I leaned against the wall so that I couldn't be pushed again. All the while I silently asked for protection. Suddenly Spirit communicated with me and in my mind's voice told me to open my hands and face them towards the sky so that I can receive protection. When my hands were closed I wasn't open to receiving protection. The elderly woman disappeared and I never saw her again.

50 — Linda Dianne

Chapter Five
The Ouija Board

52 — Linda Dianne

The Ouija Board has been used both as a toy and as a means of receiving messages or answers to questions. Many discussions have taken place as to whether or not the messages and answers received are authentic communications from the spirits of the dead.

Many Spiritualists and investigators into the occult believe that the board is a means for making direct contact with the dead and that the messages which are spelled out are from them.

Others believe that the messages are not true messages but are the result of muscular tension and unconscious direction of the hand.

Many people that I know had at least one time when they were growing up played with the Ouija Board, including me. We were not aware of the dangers and the power of our actions as we asked our questions and watched in great amazement the answers being spelled out.

Since there didn't seem to be any visible harm in using the Ouija Board, I purchased one in my later years for fun and entertainment. So I thought. My experience as an adult was quite different than that of a teenager.

Shortly after my mother passed away my teenage son and I pulled out the Ouija Board, lit some candles and decided to contact her. This was a huge mistake. How could I be so stupid? I didn't need to use the board to contact her. I already could communicate with the other side. And how could I have been so careless and not ask for protection?

This experience was a very, very bad and dangerous one. We contacted and unknowingly invited a mean, evil spirit into our home. At first the board spelled out answers to our questions (so we thought) not until the board spelled out the word *Mom* did I realize we were not connected to the spirit of my mother as she always referred to herself as *Mum*. The damage was done.

We put the board away, blew out the candles and talked about what had just happened. In the next few days like a dark cloud surrounding us, anger and depression filled our home. At night both my son and I were awakened with the smell of flesh burning and a feeling that someone was watching us. My husband had no idea that this was happening or that we had used the board.

Days went by and all the happiness in our home was buried. Things started to happen. Lights flickered on and off, there were unexplained sounds, unpleasant air and the horrible and foul smell of burning flesh. My son and I were awakened nightly to a dark shadow lingering over us and that horrible flesh burning smell.

We were even touched as we slept. A horrible invasion of a dark entity with harmful intent touching you and awakening you from a sleep is something that is not only frightening but very hard to forget. This dark evil presence would press its strong hands on my shoulders keeping me pinned down and then smelling the sickening air that forced its way into my nostrils. I could feel my heart pounding at such a pace that it felt as if it would explode. My son shared similar experiences with me, and we knew that we needed professional help. We needed someone that could rid our home of this uninvited presence.

I contacted a friend of mine who was also a psychic and she contacted another one to help us get rid of this torment. We called upon God's help and asked for the strength of his Archangels to protect us and guide us. We recited the

Lord's Prayer as my son removed the board from the house. We had already disposed of all the candles we used when we used the Ouija Board and now we had to get rid of the board permanently.

I watched through the window while my son took the board into the backyard to chop it into pieces and burn it. I continued reciting the Lord's Prayer and then I demanded the presence leave my home. "You're not welcome here, this is my home and I want you out of it right now. Leave immediately and never return. Get out, get out now, in the name of Jesus Christ, get out of my home."

The full impact of a strong force hit my chest and threw me across the room. My body hit the wall with such a thud that it caused the door to the room to slam shut. I sat there for a moment. Spirit's voice was in my mind's ear telling me not to show fear. Don't show fear. Are you kidding? I was terrified. Spirit's voice came again. Don't show fear! I got up from the floor where I had landed. "Get out now, and don't ever touch me again. Get out, this is my home and you are not welcome." A black mist formed in front of me and the smell of burning flesh was so strong that I felt I was going to vomit. The black mist was heading towards me. The words don't show fear, don't show fear, don't show fear, continued playing in my mind like a broken record. I stood still, my heart thumped loudly. Then the mist disappeared and my home was free of it.

I went to the window to watch my son break the Ouija Board. The board literally attacked my son. I watched as the board flew in the air and headed right for him. The board hit his body, flew in the air and hit him again. The board then would land on the ground and each time he tried to pick it up, it moved away from him and then on its own went into the air and threw itself at him again.

When it landed on the ground again he jumped on it causing it to crack. He then was able to use an axe and chop the board into several pieces. We then burned the pieces. The Ouija Board is a portal for all Spirits to enter. By destroying the board that we had used sealed the portal and by disposing of the candles that we lit while using the board helped to rid us and our home of negative energy.

For all that believe that using the Ouija Board for fun and entertainment please remember that it is not a toy, and it is not entertainment.

Using the board unprotected can be one of the most dangerous things you could do. All contact with the Spirit world opens a portal from their world to ours, not just the Ouija Board that I used. You may think that you are safe because nothing happened to you when you used one. An entity could have attached itself to you at the time without you knowing it, and it could be several years later that you could have an unpleasant encounter and an uninvited guest.

Chapter Six
Surprise Visitors

62 — Linda Dianne

My husband and I live in a condominium and we have both experienced surprise visitors from the other side.

Shortly after moving into our condo suite we put shelving up in both the kitchen and in our sunroom. In the sunroom the shelves displayed some of our pictures, ornaments and a few teapots from my collection. The shelves in our kitchen held several tea pots.

Some mornings we would find that the pictures on the shelves were turned facing a different direction and the tea pots and ornaments were re-arranged. The tea pots on the kitchen shelves were all facing a different direction.

These incidents lasted a few weeks until finally I just simple said "It is ok for you to visit us and stay for a short time, but it is not ok for you to touch our things and we want you to stop." Nothing was moved after that.

Another surprise visit that I had was when I was watching television alone in our family room all comfortable in a chair when suddenly the pillows on our sofa were tossed in the air and landed on the floor in front of me. It startled the heck out of me. I looked at the sofa and no one was visible, but someone was there. I said "very funny, now pick them up and put them back." Nothing happened. I made the request again, and still nothing happened so I picked up the pillows and put them back on the sofa.

One evening my husband and I were watching the television in the family room when we heard the cupboard doors in our kitchen open and shut. We listened for a while and then my husband got up and went into the kitchen.

The cupboards were closed and no one was there.

One morning we woke up and all of our lights were on. Every room was lit. The next morning just three of our lamps were on. Neither of us had turned on the lights either time.

66 — Linda Dianne

Chapter Seven
What's in the Cards?

68 — Linda Dianne

To most people the *Tara* cards are associated with psychic readings, but for me the *Rune* cards and the regular playing cards are what I use in my readings.

The word Rune itself means a "secret" or "mystery" and is associated with things whispered. Out of their Latin and Etruscan origins, and influenced by the dialects of the north Italian hill people, came the Runes. They are a twenty-four letter alphabet script created among the Germanic tribes at least two thousand years ago. This alphabet incorporated fertility symbols from prehistoric rock carvings linked to religious beliefs and ritual practices. The 24 letters were divided into 3 "families" of 8 Runes each, which were named for the Norse gods.

For centuries playing cards have been used as a means of "telling Fortunes", and many methods of reading their meaning have been developed and passed down from generation to generation.

Among practitioners of psychic reading by cards, or Cartomancy as it is called, it is generally believed that the cards should not be consulted too frequently.

There are two major systems for using the ordinary pack of bridge or playing cards for readings. One system makes use of the entire deck of 52 cards. The other uses only 32 cards, the twos, threes, fours, fives and sixes being discarded. This is the system that I use.

My grandmother used regular playing cards and the fascination with them being used for more than a game was of interest to me. I tried to remember how she laid the cards on the table and what each one meant. I even bought a book on how to do readings with the playing cards.

To my surprise, I found that I didn't need a book to learn the meaning of the cards. I already knew that cards were just a visual for the person you are reading and a guide to concentrate on the energies of the person you are doing the reading for. I was reading energies not cards. As I handed the cards to my client to shuffle and return them to me I immediately was able to pick up their energy from the cards. This energy was like the ON switch for the visions I would see. How amazing! I could actually see into the life of someone else. Wow what a gift! What an incredible gift! This is not to say that the cards only play a visual role in the reading, they are a powerful means of identifying direction and receiving energy. Some Readers rely mainly on the cards, what order they are placed in, and so on. For me, I use cards as a medium to collect energy.

When I finally felt comfortable enough in my ability to give readings with the cards it took me quite a while to believe in myself and that the messages I was receiving and relaying to my clients were accurate and not something my imagination created. When I received validation of something that I said, my confidence strengthened and I enjoyed helping others with guidance from my Spirit Guide Jooseth, along with my wonderful team of angels and guides.

I started to give readings in a small Tea Room in the east end of Toronto every Saturday. This experience gave me more confidence and strengthened my psychic awareness to a deeper level. I was really helping people. They would come to the Tea room with sad and puzzled faces and sit down in front of me for a reading. Each one I gave a reading to left with confidence and a smile. I was able to help them with whatever was bothering them. I helped them understand the confusion surrounding them. I gave them hope and guided them on their journey.

Strange Normal — 73

During one of my readings a vision of an empty coffin appeared in front of me. I wasn't sure if this meant the end of something, or the passing of someone, or that the client was going to die. I ignored the coffin and quickly and silently asked my Spirit guide Jooseth for a symbol of something more specific than a coffin. It appeared again, but this time in the coffin was a baby. I was totally confused now. Did this mean that this is the end of something and a beginning of something, or the death of a baby or unborn child? I continued with the reading, confused as to what the message about the coffin was, until another vision entered my mind's eye. Images appeared that I could associate with. First dark clouds drifted by and then sunshine. This message I understood. The darkness or dark clouds surrounding my client were soon to be in the past and a brighter future was on the way.

During another reading I began to hear a choir sing, and in front of me were hospital beds filled with patients. The client was a woman who wanted to know about her son who soon would be off to University. I couldn't see her son or a University only a hallway full of patients in hospital beds and the choir kept singing. So I told her that I saw a hospital full of patients, I didn't see her son, but I did see a choir, I didn't say that I could hear the choir just that I could see it. She smiled and said that her husband was a Doctor and she sang in a choir that visited patients that were in a long term care facility. This was a validation from Spirit. By the end of the reading she received information about her concerns.

It took some time to communicate with Spirit in a manner that we both could adapt to. I needed visions/symbols that related to me so that I can interpret them to give accurate readings. Now when I don't understand the vision or symbol I just tell my client what I see and usually it means something to them.

I was soon invited to participate in a

psychic fair at the Tea room. There would be several psychics giving readings and I would be one of them. This was indeed a challenge. Each reading was to be only 20 minutes and the next customer would be ready for their 20 minute reading.

I was able to give readings to 20 people at the fair and I met some amazing psychics. When the event was over the psychics chatted for a while reflecting on the day's event and the many people that attended. Each of us had the opportunity to read some of the same people and although we didn't share what we saw we did however share the difficulties when dealing with someone that doesn't respond to anything you have to say until the very end of the reading. This really puts pressure on the Reader. If feedback isn't given during the reading than it is very confusing for the Reader to know if they are giving you an accurate reading.

So many people have the attitude

that because we are psychic we know and see everything. This is not the case. We need to know if the messages we are receiving are for you, or for someone in your family, or for someone you know. We need validation as much as the person receiving the reading.

At the end of the day I was completely and utterly exhausted. I was emotionally drained and worse than that, like a sponge I absorbed everyone's energy. All that negative energy bundled itself up and attached itself to me like a backpack full of bricks.I needed help. How do I get rid of this energy? I contacted a psychic friend to help me get rid of this negative energy and to help me always be protected so that this doesn't happen again.

The solution was easy. I called upon Archangel Michael. I asked Michael to be my warrior and to protect me from all negative, harmful, dark and evil energies. I asked him to cleanse my mind and body of the harmful energy I had absorbed. I call upon Archangel Michael everyday to be my warrior and to protect me, and he does.

Working with the Spirit world used to be very challenging and confusing for me. Since this was going to be part of my life I needed to learn more about it. I attended several conferences and seminars and read countless books to learn more about the connection between this world and the unseen world. I attended seminars held by Sylvia Browne a world renowned psychic, John Holland who is one of Canada's most sought after psychics and Dr. Doreen Virtue known for her healing techniques and Angel therapy. It was her seminar that changed my life by introducing me to working with the Archangels. I also attended a workshop presented by the Rescue Mediums who make house calls to help wayward spirits. At this workshop I learned about vibrations, energy levels and how to safely help a trapped Spirit into the light.

I also studied hypnosis to learn how the conscious and unconscious minds receive messages. I received my Hypnosis certification and am now a practitioner of Hypnotherapy.

Communications with the other side are now very easy for me and a consistent and *normal* part of my life.

Chapter Eight
Tea Leaves and Tea Cups

80 — Linda Dianne

The practice of looking into a teacup to discover, from the shapes, left by the tea leaves, what is to happen in the future is very old. Thousands of years ago people believed that ringing bells would drive away evil. This led to the belief that one could find inside a bell tokens of the future. So men began to study the inside of bells and to predict the future from what they found there.

Then the ancient Chinese realized that a teacup was much like a bell inverted. So they began to study the inside of tea cups from which the tea had been drunk and in which a few leaves were left in interesting patterns and forms. Now after many centuries, the reading of tea leaves in order to predict the future is practiced throughout the world.

Reading tea leaves is a favourite psychic talent of mine. There is so much hidden amongst the leaves that sometimes it may take 1 hour to complete a reading. Just as I did so many years ago when staring at the clouds and watching them change shape, I do the same when reading the leaves. It may sound strange because the leaves unlike clouds do not move or change shape, but when I am viewing the leaves they do.

The type of tea cup and saucer are very important for an accurate reading. They must be white, smooth and with no design. If you try to read from a coloured cup, or one with flowers or other designs it is very difficult to see the leaves. A white background makes it possible to read tea leaves no matter what type of tea leaves you are reading. Before a reading can take place the client must drink the tea first so that their energy is contained in the cup. If desired you can add a little milk to the tea but no sugar, honey, lemon or anything else.

Strange Normal — 85

what I saw? I had to control my urge to hug her, and hold back the tears that were filling my eyes. I needed help, so that I could help her or at least try.

I closed my eyes and asked God to help me. I wanted to say the right things. I wanted to really reach her spirit and let her know she is loved and special but would she believe me? *Clairaudience* kicked in again and I was guided by Spirit to help her. I told her that I could see that she had suffered abuse, both sexual and physical. I certainly did not want to tell her what I saw. She started to cry and I wasn't prepared for that.

Through the help of Spirit I was able to change the energy around her from darkness to light and the visions I was now seeing were of joy and strength and peace for her. She left the Tea room with a smile and gave me a hug and a $5 tip. She said she hadn't smiled in a long time, and had given up on her life. I asked her what made her come to a psychic and she said she saw the tea room and just entered. She had not planned to have a reading but somehow she felt she had to.

That same day I did another tea leaf reading for a man that came to the Tea room to have a bite to eat. He saw me there and asked for a reading. He drank his tea and handed me the cup. The visions began but this time in symbols and I had to figure out what they meant. Were the symbols something that I could identify with, or were they something associated with him? In the bottom of his cup I could see a bouquet of daffodils. Big, bright yellow daffodils, and under the bouquet was the letter C. Now to some people daffodils mean that Spring is here, and sometimes daffodils are just daffodils.

To me daffodils remind me of cancer as it is the flower that is sold to raise funds for cancer research. An initial in a tea cup can represent a person, a place, or a thing. I had to quickly interpret what I was seeing.

I asked him if someone he knows had cancer and had recently passed on. I told him I saw the letter C. He told me that his step-mother Catherine had died of cancer just two weeks ago. As the reading continued I kept seeing a turtle. This turtle was real, and old and big and muddy. I ignored the vision of the turtle because I wasn't sure what it meant.

The turtle wouldn't go away instead it got larger blocking out the other visions. I gave in and finally told my client that for some reason I keep seeing a turtle and asked if that meant anything to him. With a smile he told me that his ancestors came from Turtle Island. This was a validation from Spirit that I was receiving and delivering accurate messages.

When interpreting symbols it is a little confusing to know if the symbol is something you identify with or the person you are reading. After doing so many readings now, I don't question what I see, if the symbol is there and I have to think about it than it clearly is not associated with me and I just mention what I see.

When I got home from the Tea room, after such an emotional day, I asked God to take away this psychic gift because I didn't want it anymore. It wasn't a gift, it was "Pandora's box" and I didn't want to see violence, rapes and sadness. I just wanted to be normal. I didn't want to know so much about other people and the lives they lead. I just wanted to help people not re-arrange their lives and view their stories. Couldn't someone else do this? Give me another way to help people. The answer I received wasn't what I wanted to hear.

Spirit spoke to me in a strong voice in my head and told me that all I had to do was ask for the visions to be calmer. So I did. I asked that the visions be of only what is necessary for me to see. I don't need to see a rape to learn that someone was violated you can tell me that in words not pictures. I sat crying on my bed for a while. The visions of that young girl wouldn't go away and God wasn't going to take away my psychic abilities. So I sat there, crying and asking for help. I called upon Archangel Michael and I called out to God for a hug from heaven. I said that I was sorry I got angry because I was frustrated. And that I would try again to use my abilities to help others.

The visions were and are calmer and I continued to do readings at the Tea room until it went out of business and then I began giving readings in my home, which I still do

One of the readings I did in my home was for two sisters. One of the sisters wanted a reading but wanted her sister to sit in on it with her. I was reading tea leaves again, and as I looked into the cup and began to read a vision of a bunch of bananas floated in front of me.

I ignored the bananas but they didn't ignore me. They got bigger and blocked my viewing. Since the symbol of a banana meant nothing to me the only option I had was to mention to the client that I can see bananas and asked if that meant anything to her. Both the sisters started to laugh and told me that their mother always eats bananas but lately she will cut one in half and eat it and put the other half in a cupboard. Often they had to check the cupboards to find the other half of the banana. Another validation received from Spirit.

Chapter Nine
The Crystal Ball

92 — Linda Dianne

Crystal-gazing is an ancient and widely practiced art. Through its use many strange things have happened. Crimes have been solved, lost articles found, hidden facts in the lives of people have been uncovered, and unrealized aspects of one's relationships with others have been revealed.

Although crystal-gazing has been used with some remarkable success in piecing together the facts of the past, its chief use both by professional seers and others is to look into the future and discover what is about to happen or what may happen unless precautions are taken.

The first requirement for successful crystal-gazing is for the person to be highly sensitive and receptive. The second prerequisite is to have a clear crystal in which to gaze. The crystal should be the size of a baseball or even a bit larger.

There are several ways to use the crystal ball and some psychics will not let anyone touch their crystal ball because of the energies it amplifies. Crystal is used in communications with the Spirit world because of its ability to amplify angelic energy, just as the crystals in watches and radios amplify other forms of energy.

Crystals are a wonderful tool for connecting with the angelic realm. They act like megaphones by increasing the signal strength of communications and healing energies that our angels are sending us.

I received my crystal ball as a gift. When I do readings, cards or tea leaves I usually have the ball centered in the reading room to enhance the energy. When I actually do readings with the crystal ball I have my client hold the crystal with both hands for a few moments and then I replace their hands with mine on the crystal and read their energies. *Clairvoyance* (clear seeing) and *Clairsentience* (clear sensing) are used with the Crystal Ball.

Sometimes the crystal ball will change colour from its beautiful pink to a blue. This has happened several times during readings and I have no idea why this happens. When the reading is finished the crystal returns to its natural pink shade.

During one of my readings using the crystal ball I saw a cat slowly walking around the ball. It just kept walking, slower and slower. When I told my client that I could see a cat but it seemed like it was in the spirit world and moving very slowly. He told me that his cat had passed away a few months earlier. He had the cat for a number of years and it actually died of old age. In the final days of the cat's life on earth it walked slower and slower. That was the first time that I had seen a vision of an animal that had crossed over.

During another reading I saw an elderly woman lying in a bed with a homemade quilt on the end of the bed. Then I saw Doctors and nurses and then a flashing red light. When I mentioned this to my client, her eyes filled with tears and she told me that her grandmother was very ill and not expected to live much longer. A few days later she contacted me to tell me that her grandmother had passed away. She was taken to the hospital in an ambulance.

In another Crystal Ball reading my hands began to ache. I had to let go of the ball for a moment because the pain was so severe. I touched the ball again and pain shot up my left arm and then stopped. My client told me that he had suffered a minor stroke a couple of weeks earlier.

Chapter Ten
Automatic Writing (psychography)

98 — *Linda Dianne*

Automatic writing is a channelling technique for your higher self or another entity to use your hands to write messages or information. The phenomena was investigated by psychologists during the 1800's and 1900's . According to their theory the source of automatic writing material is in the subconscious.

My experience with automatic writing is limited but it has been very comforting. I was able to contact my brother who passed away several years ago. I have also contacted my parents, my grandmother and others.

In my first book "Hugs From Heaven" I detailed my conversations with both my brother and my mother. As I am not really comfortable yet with someone else using my hand as an instrument to write messages, I rely on other techniques to receive information from my guides.

Afterword

102 — Linda Dianne

Each morning I take the time to meditate. Sometimes it may be for only 10 minutes, and depending on my schedule for the day it may take 1 to 2 hours.

Every day I continue to ask for guidance and protection and I give thanks to God and all of God's messengers. Everyone should take the time to use their inner guidance and to give yourself permission to let it assist, guide, and show you any and everything that's possible. It will help you navigate your life's path, and it will be a constant companion for your soul's journey.

We all have all the tools we need to live an intuitive life and tap into the inner guidance system that's always been with us—no matter how often you've ignored it or didn't pay attention to its voice.

The intent of this book was to break down some of the perceived barriers associated with what is known as "normal" and "strange". Our gifts/talents may differ but we are all blessed, and loved. My strength is my psychic abilities and I use them only for the true purpose of helping others.

My reward in doing so is seeing and knowing that I have made a positive difference in the lives of those that seek my direction.

May your life be filled with love, abundance, and happiness.

CPSIA information can be obtained at www.ICGtesting.com
Printed in the USA
LVOW010043081011

249610LV00004B/1/P